First published in Great Britain by Egmont Books
239 Kensington High Street
London W12 8NU

Copyright 2001 by Disney Enterprises, Inc.

ISBN 0 7497 4617 3

Printed and bound in Great Britain

10 9 8 7 6 5 4 3 2 1

AS THE SEA RAGES OVER THE DOMED CITY, LEAVING VIRTUALLY NO TRACE OF ITS EXISTENCE.

THWMOOSSSHHH

WASHINGTON, D.C., 1914. DEEP IN THE BOILER ROOM, MILO THATCH REHEARSES HIS ADDRESS TO THE MUSEUM'S BOARD OF DIRECTORS...

GENTLEMEN, WE'VE ALL HEARD THE LEGEND OF ATLANTIS, A CONTINENT SOMEWHERE IN THE MID-ATLANTIC THAT WAS HOME TO AN ADVANCED CIVILISATION. THEY HAD ELECTRICITY, ADVANCED MEDICINE, EVEN THE POWER OF FLIGHT!

ATLANTIS POSSESSED A POWER SOURCE OF SOME KIND THAT ENABLED THEM TO ACHIEVE ALL OF THOSE THINGS AND MORE...

CLICK

RRRINNNG

EXCUSE ME, GENTLEMEN.

I PROPOSE THAT WE FIND ATLANTIS, FIND THAT POWER SOURCE, AND BRING IT BACK TO THE SURFACE!

CARTOGRAPHY AND LINGUISTICS. MILO THATCH SPEAKING...! BOILER PROBLEM? YEAH, YEAH, JUST A SECOND.

BLAH BLAH BLAH BBLAH

WHACH

IS THAT BETTER? YOU'RE WELCOME. UH, BYE.

DEAR MR THATCH: THIS IS TO INFORM YOU THAT YOUR MEETING TODAY HAS BEEN MOVED UP FROM 4.30 P.M. TO 3.30 P.M. DUE TO YOUR ABSENCE, THE BOARD HAS VOTED TO REJECT YOUR PROPOSAL. HAVE A NICE WEEKEND. MR. HARCOURT'S OFFICE.

THEY CAN'T DO THIS TO ME!

I SWEAR THAT YOUNG THATCH GETS CRAZIER EVERY YEAR.

IF I EVER HEAR THE WORD "ATLANTIS" AGAIN, I'LL STEP IN FRONT OF A BUS.

HA, HA! I'LL PUSH YOU!

MEMBERS OF THE BOARD! UH, WAIT!

WAIT, MR HARCOURT! SIR, I HAVE NEW EVIDENCE!

THIS MUSEUM FUNDS SCIENTIFIC EXPEDITIONS BASED ON **FACTS**, NOT LEGENDS AND FOLKLORE. BESIDES, WE NEED YOU **HERE**. WITH WINTER COMING, THAT BOILER'S GOING TO NEED A LOT OF ATTENTION.

BUT I CAN **PROVE ATLANTIS EXISTS**! THERE'S A JOURNAL – **THE SHEPHERD'S JOURNAL** – IN ICELAND! IF YOU DON'T LISTEN TO ME, I'LL...

YOU'LL WHAT? RUIN YOUR CAREER LIKE YOUR **CRAZY GRANDFATHER**?

TAKE A TROLLEY TO THE POTOMAC AND JUMP IN. MAYBE THE COLD WATER WILL CLEAR YOUR HEAD!

THAT EVENING, **MILO** FINDS A MYSTERIOUS VISITOR IN HIS APARTMENT...

WHO ARE YOU? HOW DID YOU GET IN HERE?

MILO JAMES THATCH? MY NAME IS **HELGA SINCLAIR**. MY EMPLOYER HAS A MOST INTRIGUING PROPOSITION FOR YOU...

KRAA-B BOOOM

MR. WHITMORE DOES NOT LIKE TO BE KEPT WAITING. AND RELAX, HE DOESN'T BITE...OFTEN.

TH-THAT'S MY **GRANDPA!**

FINEST EXPLORER I EVER MET!

PRESTON WHITMORE. IT'S A PLEASURE TO MEET YOU, MILO.

JOIN ME IN A LITTLE YOGA?

UH, NO. THANK YOU. DID YOU REALLY KNOW MY GRANDFATHER?

WE STAYED CLOSE FRIENDS TO THE END OF HIS DAYS...EVEN DRAGGED ME ALONG ON SOME OF HIS DARN FOOL EXPEDITIONS.

SHOULD I BE WONDERING WHY I'M HERE?

LOOK ON THAT TABLE. IT'S FOR YOU.

HE SAID IF ANYTHING HAPPENED TO HIM, I SHOULD GIVE IT TO YOU WHEN YOU WERE READY.

IT... CAN'T BE...

IT'S THE **SHEPHERD'S JOURNAL**!

MR. WHITMORE, THIS JOURNAL IS THE KEY TO FINDING THE LOST CONTINENT OF ATLANTIS! I'LL SHOW THE MUSEUM! I WILL **MAKE** THEM BELIEVE ME NOW!

LIKE YOU DID TODAY?

YES! NO! HOW DID YOU KNOW? NEVER MIND, I WILL FIND **ATLANTIS** ON MY OWN IF I HAVE TO **RENT A ROWBOAT**!

CONGRATULATIONS, MILO! THAT'S **EXACTLY** WHAT I WANTED TO HEAR! FORGET THE ROWBOAT, SON. WE'LL TRAVEL IN **STYLE**!

CLICK

YOU SEE, MILO, YOUR GRANDPA WAS A GREAT MAN. THOSE BUFFOONS AT THE MUSEUM DRAGGED HIM DOWN AND MADE HIM A LAUGHING STOCK. HE DIED A BROKEN MAN. IF YOU COULD BRING BACK ONE SHRED OF PROOF, THAT WOULD BE ENOUGH FOR ME.

BUT MR. WHITMORE, YOU'RE GONNA NEED A CREW – ENGINEERS AND GEOLOGISTS...

FWEENNN...CLICK...TWICK

GOT THE BEST...**GAETAN MOLIERE**, GEOLOGY AND EXCAVATIONS. **VINCHENZO SANTORINI**, DEMOLITIONS. **AUDREY RAMIREZ**, ENGINEER. THEY'RE THE SAME CREW THAT BROUGHT THE **JOURNAL** BACK FROM ICELAND.

I KNEW IT! I KNEW IT! THIS IS FOR REAL!

9

MOVE IT, PEOPLE! SOMETIME TODAY WOULD BE NICE! C'MON! EVERYBODY GRAB A SEAT AND BUCKLE IN!

LIEUTENANT, GET US OUT OF HERE!

I'M WORKING ON IT!

CRRUMMMBLE

HANG ON!

WHERE TO, MR. THATCH?

WE'RE LOOKING FOR A BIG CREVICE OF SOME KIND.

THERE! UP AHEAD!

ALL CRAFT MAKE YOUR MARK TWENTY DEGREES DOWN ANGLE!

VINNY AND I ARE RIGHT BEHIND YOU!

WITH ONLY ONE AQUA-EVAC VEHICLE AND ONE SUBPOD LEFT, THE REMAINING CREW SURFACES IN AN AIR POCKET.

SEVEN HOURS AGO, WE STARTED THIS EXPEDITION WITH 200 OF THE FINEST MEN AND WOMEN I'VE EVER KNOWN. WE'RE ALL THAT'S LEFT. WE HAVE A CRISIS ON OUR HANDS BUT WE'VE ALWAYS COME THROUGH, AND I SEE NO REASON TO CHANGE THAT POLICY.

LOOKS LIKE ALL OUR CHANCES FOR SURVIVAL REST WITH YOU, MR. THATCH. YOU AND THAT LITTLE BOOK.

WE'RE ALL GONNA DIE.

OKAY, PEOPLE, SADDLE UP! LIEUTENANT, I WANT THIS CONVOY MOVING FIVE MINUTES AGO.

CAN YOU DRIVE A TRUCK?

PFFT HA, HA! OF COURSE I CAN DRIVE A TRUCK! AH, SURE, YOU'VE GOT YOUR STEERING AND YOUR GAS AND YOUR BRAKE...AND OF COURSE, THIS...METAL... UH, LOOKING THING...

OKAY, SO IT WAS A BUMPER CAR AT CONEY ISLAND! BUT IT'S STILL THE SAME BASIC PRINCIPLE!

A SHORT TIME LATER...

RRROOOIMWW

OOPS. SORRY.

YOU DIDN'T JUST DRINK THAT, DID YOU? THAT'S NITRO GLYCERINE! DON'T MOVE!

BOOOM

HAAHAHAHA HAHA

UNFORTUNATELY, MILO HASN'T EXACTLY ENDEARED HIMSELF TO THE CREW...

...AND HIS ONLY FRIEND IN THIS DISTANT WORLD IS **THE SHEPHERD'S JOURNAL.**

GOOD NIGHT! THIS HAS GOT TO BE HALF A MILE HIGH! IT MUST HAVE TAKEN HUNDREDS...NO *PFFT* THOUSANDS OF YEARS TO CARVE OUT THIS THING.

KAFWOOOOM

HEY LOOK, I MADE A BRIDGE. AND IT ONLY TOOK ME TEN SECONDS, ELEVEN, TOPS.

LOOKS LIKE WE HAVE A LITTLE ROAD BLOCK. READY TO DIG, MOLE?

IT WOULD BE MY PLEASURE.

ROARR RRRUMBLE

COUGH AARGH!

CACHUNKA CHU

SOMETHING WRONG WITH YOUR NECK?

YEAH – I MUST HAVE HURT IT WHEN...

YAHHH! GAHHH!

CRRRICK

BETTER?

YEAH...HEY, WHERE'D YOU LEARN TO DO THAT?

AN ARAPAHO MEDICINE MAN...MY FATHER WAS AN ARMY MEDIC. HE SETTLED DOWN IN KANSAS AFTER HE MET MY MOTHER. I GOT A SHEEPSKIN FROM HOWARD U. AND A BEARSKIN FROM OL' IRON CLOUD.

AREN'T YOU GONNA PITCH YOUR TENT?

AH, I DID. GUESS I'M A LITTLE RUSTY. I HAVEN'T BEEN CAMPING SINCE LAST TIME GRANDPA TOOK ME.

I NEVER GOT TO MEET YOUR GRANDFATHER. WHAT WAS HE LIKE?

WELL, MY PARENTS DIED WHEN I WAS LITTLE, SO HE WAS LIKE A FATHER TO ME. ONCE WHEN I WAS EIGHT, I FOUND AN ARROWHEAD IN A STREAM. WELL, YOU'D A THOUGHT I FOUND A LOST CIVILISATION, THE WAY GRANDPA CARRIED ON ABOUT IT.

WHEN I WAS OLDER, I REALISED THE ARROWHEAD WAS JUST SOME COMPRESSED SHALE.

WELL, MY DAD ALWAYS WANTED SONS – ONE TO RUN HIS MACHINE SHOP AND ONE TO BECOME MIDDLEWEIGHT BOXING CHAMPION.

SO MY SISTER'S 24 AND 0 WITH A SHOT AT THE TITLE, AND I'M SAVING UP SO MY POPPY AND I CAN OPEN ANOTHER SHOP.

WELL, AS FAR AS "ME" GOES, I JUST LIKE TO BLOW STUFF UP.

COME ON, VINNY, TELL THE KID THE TRUTH.

MY FAMILY OWNED A FLOWER SHOP. ONE DAY I'M MAKING CORSAGES. AND EVERYBODY, THEY COME, "WHERE IS IT?" "WILL IT MATCH MY DRESS?" IT'S A NIGHTMARE.

ANYWAY, THERE'S THIS GAS LEAK NEXT DOOR, AND BOOM! NO MORE CHINESE LAUNDRY. IT WAS LIKE A SIGN. I FOUND MYSELF WITH THAT BOOM.

WHAT'S MOLE'S STORY?

TRUST ME, YOU DON'T WANT TO KNOW.

HEH, HEH.

AS THE CREW SLEEPS, MYSTERIOUS VISITORS EXPLORE THE CAMP...

FLUTTER FLUTTER FLUTTER

THEY FLEE WHEN MILO STEPS OUT FOR A STROLL.

MILO INADVERTENTLY SHINES A LIGHT ON SOME PECULIAR FIREFLIES.

...AND TO HIS HORROR, THE FIREFLIES START A BLAZE!

FIRE! FIRE! FIRE!

THATCH, GO BACK TO BE-!?

GET SOME WATER ON THAT FIRE!

NO TIME! GET US INTO THOSE CAVES! MOVE IT, MOVE IT, MOVE IT!

WHEN THE FIREFLIES PELT THE FUEL TRUCK WITH FLAMES...

THEIR HIVE FALLS...

CAUSING THE BRIDGE TO EXPLODE!

THE TRUCKS SLIDE BACKWARDS OFF THE BRIDGE...

NO! NO! NO!

AND HURL DOWN A PITCH-BLACK CHASM!

HOLY CATS! WHO ARE THESE GUYS?

THEY GOTTA BE ATLANTEANS!

WHAT?! THAT'S IMPOSSIBLE!

I'VE SEEN THIS BACK IN THE DAKOTA. THEY CAN SMELL FEAR JUST BY LOOKIN' AT YA. SO KEEP QUIET.

LEB EH-SEH-NEK DUPP-DOO-WEH-REN-TOAP? LUHT SULL-DOO-PEH-NEKH DUPP?*

*WHO ARE YOU AND WHERE DO YOU COME FROM?

LEB EH-SEH-NEKH DUPP-DOO-WEH-REN-TOAP? LUHT SULL-DOO-PEH-NEKH DUPP?*

PRAH-WHT-TEM DUHN-GU-NUHG MOH-KHIN YOO-GEHB-LEH-TOAT BET KAH-PEH-REH KIHK.*

*WHO ARE YOU AND WHERE DO YOU COME FROM?

*YOUR MANNER OF SPEECH IS STRANGE TO ME

PARLEZ-VOUS FRANCAIS?

OUI, MONSIEUR!

THEY SPEAK MY LANGUAGE!

PARDON, MADEMOISELLE? AH, VOULEZ-VOUS... BUZZ... BUZZ...BUZZ...

BOFF

OOH! I LIKE HER!

HMMM. 'BOUT TIME SOMEONE HIT HIM. I'M JUST SORRY IT WASN'T ME!

GUTENTAG! WIEGEHTS! CIAO! SHALOM! SALUT! GRUBSTE! YASU! NEEHOWMA! LEHOBO!

HOW DO THEY KNOW ALL THESE DIALECTS?

THEIR LANGUAGE MUST BE BASED ON A ROOT DIALECT, JUST LIKE THE TOWER OF BABEL.

WELL, MAYBE ENGLISH IS IN THERE SOMEWHERE.

30

33

41

ZEEOOOM

'KABAMM

ROURKE'S TROOPERS ATTACK!

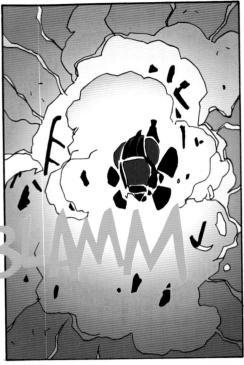

VINNY, NEW PLAN. YOU AND ME – WE'RE GONNA BE DECOYS. AUDREY, SWEET...

WE'RE ON IT!

I THOUGHT YOU SAID THIS THING COULD CUT THROUGH A FEMUR IN 28 SECONDS!

LESS TALK, MORE SAW!

MILO FLIES BY THE BALLOON AND LEAPS ONTO IT!

RRIP

WE'RE LOSING ALTITUDE! LIGHTEN THE LOAD!

THAT'S IT, UNLESS SOMEONE WANTS TO JUMP.

LADIES FIRST!

42

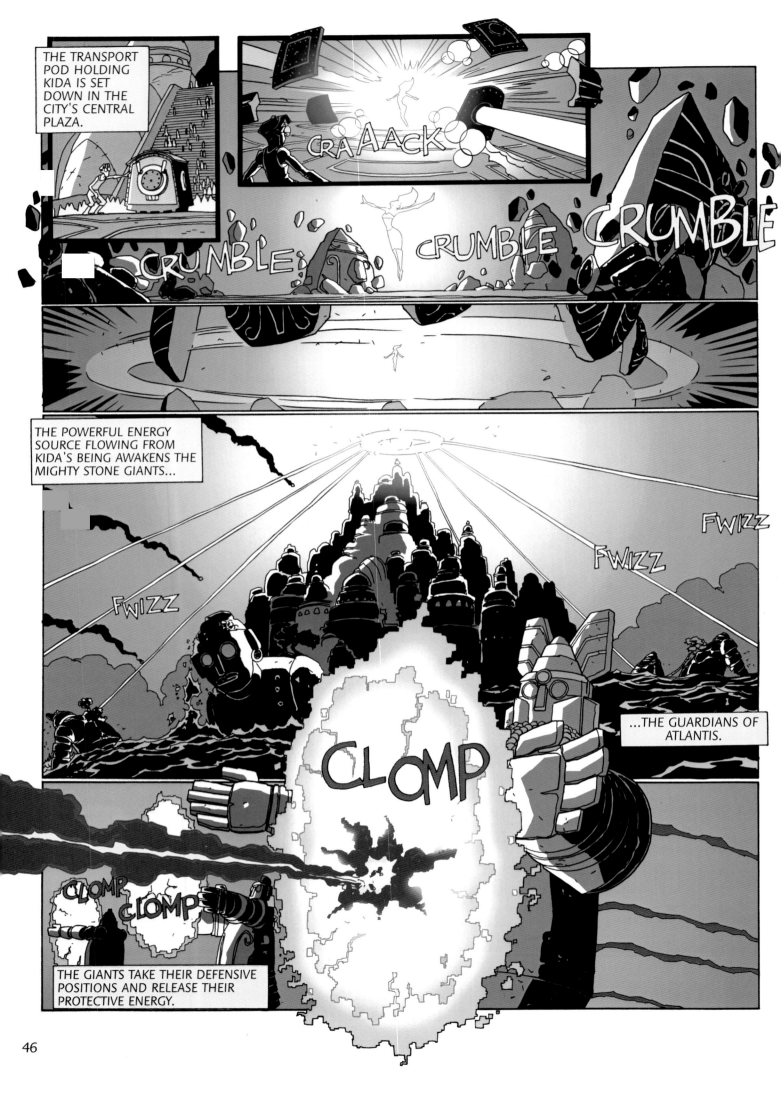

THE TRANSPORT POD HOLDING KIDA IS SET DOWN IN THE CITY'S CENTRAL PLAZA.

CRAAACK

CRUMBLE CRUMBLE CRUMBLE

THE POWERFUL ENERGY SOURCE FLOWING FROM KIDA'S BEING AWAKENS THE MIGHTY STONE GIANTS...

FWIZZ FWIZZ FWIZZ

...THE GUARDIANS OF ATLANTIS.

CLOMP

CLOMP CLOMP

THE GIANTS TAKE THEIR DEFENSIVE POSITIONS AND RELEASE THEIR PROTECTIVE ENERGY.

FA-WHOOOSH

CRACK

CRACK CRACK

THE ENERGY SHIELD MAKES THE LAVA HARDEN AND CRUMBLE INTO DUST!

CRUMBLE CRUMBLE

MILO...

FROM THE CLOUDS OF RISING STEAM. KIDA REURNS.

WITH ATLANTIS RETURNING TO ITS FORMER GLORY...

... THE CREW PREPARES TO SAY FAREWELL.

GIFTS OF TREASURE ARE LOADED INTO THE HUGE SHIP.